BOSTON'S
SECRET SPACES

BOSTON'S
SECRET SPACES

50 Hidden Corners In and Around the Hub

The Boston Globe

Foreword by Robin Brown

Guilford, Connecticut

Copyright © 2009 by The Boston Globe

Text design by Sheryl P. Kober

Library of Congress Cataloging-in-Publication Data
Boston's secret spaces : 50 hidden corners in and around the Hub / the
Boston Globe ; introduction by Robin Brown.
    p. cm.
 ISBN 978-0-7627-5062-7
 1. Historic sites—Massachusetts—Boston. 2. Historic buildings—
Massachusetts—Boston. 3. Curiosities and wonders—Massachusetts—
Boston. 4. Boston (Mass.)—Buildings, structures, etc. 5. Historic
sites—Massachusetts—Boston—Pictorial works. 6. Historic buildings—
Massachusetts—Boston—Pictorial works. 7. Boston (Mass.)—Pictorial
works. 8. Boston Region (Mass.)—Pictorial works. 9. Boston (Mass.)—
Description and travel. 10. Boston Region (Mass.)—Description and
travel. I. Globe Newspaper Co.
 F73.37.B7745 2009
 917.44'610444—dc22
                                                                2008050391

Printed in China
10 9 8 7 6 5 4 3 2 1

Contents

My Secret Spaces—and Yours   ix
Foreword by Robin Brown

A City and Its Roots   xi
Introduction by David Beard

Inside Bob Kraft's Box   1
Gillette Stadium

Where Plants Propagate   2
Dana Greenhouse, Arnold Arboretum

Checking into a "Haunted" Hotel   5
The Omni Parker House Hotel

Beneath the Ether Dome   6
Massachusetts General Hospital

Inspecting the Gilding   9
Massachusetts State House

Inside the Green Igloo   10
Boston Public Garden

Helping the Planes Land   13
Logan International Airport

Meeting the Lady in Black   14
Fort Warren, Georges Island

Lighting the Lanterns   17
Old North Church

Where the Wild Things Are   18
Harvard Museum of Natural History

Where Time Unwinds   21
The Old State House

Where Brides Cry   22
Priscilla of Boston

In the Eye of the Storm   25
The National Weather Service

To the Center of the Earth   26
The Mapparium at the Mary Baker Eddy Library

Sleeping at a Crime Scene   29
Lizzie Borden Bed & Breakfast

CONTENTS

Looking through Tom Brady's Locker   30
Gillette Stadium

Hanging Out over Fenway   33
The Hood America A-60 Plus Lightship

Training Puppies in Prison   34
Northeastern Correctional Center

Inside the Green Monster   37
Fenway Park

Making Your Own Electrical Storm   38
*The Van de Graaff Generator at the Museum
of Science*

Bridging the Gender Gap   41
Jacque's Cabaret

Swimming with the Sharks   42
New England Aquarium

Working for a Scoop   45
Breyers Ice Cream Plant

Preparing Potions   46
The Cat, The Crow, and The Crown

Skulking amid the Sculls   49
Weld Boathouse

Building a Mystery   50
The Massachusetts Grand Lodge

Finding Respite   53
Bigelow Chapel, Mount Auburn Cemetery

Beneath the Tobin Bridge   54
Massport Bridge Administration

Working the Barre   57
The Boston Ballet

Basking in the Glow   58
The Citgo Sign

Composing the Roar of the Greasepaint   61
Blue Man Group

Learning from Patient Patients   62
Brigham and Women's Hospital

A Lil' Bit o' NASA   65
Northeastern University

Inside a Meat Locker   66
T. F. Kinnealey & Co.

The "Real" Top of the Hub   69
The Prudential Tower

Watching for Fire   70
Department of Conservation and Recreation

Dining with Legends   73
Locke-Ober

Saddling Up with the Mounted Police   74
Boston Police Department

Grounding the Zakim   77
Boston Sand and Gravel Co.

Meeting Eugene O'Neill   78
Shelton Hall, Boston University

Cruising in the State Police Corvette   81
Nashoba Valley Technical Institute

Inspecting the E. Howard & Co. Clock   82
The Marriott Custom House

Going Nowhere on the Red Line   85
The Massachusetts Bay Transportation Authority

Off the Ice:
Inside the Bruins' Locker Room   86
TD Banknorth Garden

Riding WBZ's Traffic Helicopter   89
Above Greater Boston

The Secret Gardens of Beacon Hill   90
Beacon Hill Garden Club

Exploring Acela's Cockpit   93
Amtrak's Acela Train

Feeding the Lions   94
Franklin Park Zoo

Raising a Glass   97
Cheers Pub

Visiting a Nuclear Reactor   98
Massachusetts Institute of Technology

Credits   100

My Secret Spaces—and Yours

Newly arrived from England and eager to learn about Boston, I was fortunate to see my first baseball game at Fenway Park the way it ought to be observed—sitting in a private box next to the grande dame of Boston baseball, Jean Yawkey. Under-jeweled and without ostentation, she sipped chardonnay and smoked cigarettes with those full inhales and talking exhales that remind you of Lauren Bacall in *To Have and Have Not*. I knew at once I was in the presence of the essence of Boston.

As a hotelier, I have enjoyed access to the inner sanctums of many great cities of the world. None of them matches Boston. As the Standells once sang, "Boston, you're my home." (And they weren't originally from Boston, either.)

It takes a while, however, to know this city. You will not find the bustle of New York, the flash of Dubai, or the honky-tonk of New Orleans. Boston is subtle, a beautiful woman with a soft voice. When you're not looking, she steals your heart.

In these pages, *The Boston Globe* and Boston.com have done the homework for us by scouting the secret settings that make Boston special. Like plants that send roots deep into soil, we Bostonians burrow contentedly in our own city, in our own spaces, and in our own places. We thrive, too, for Boston is a city aflower in the loam that enriches life—education, history, politics, sports, art, music, and libraries. And much of it is like Mrs. Yawkey: without ostentation.

One day, I ascended within the spire of the Park Street Church, where the view—and the perspective—proved breathtaking. Seen from above, Boston unfolds magnificently—the narrow, winding streets where liberty in America was born. Surrounding it are neighborhoods with a rich blend of cultures that make Boston more vibrant, more exciting, and more optimistic today than ever.

All of us have our own secret spots in Boston. Some are obvious—who can miss the Bunker Hill Monument?—but others need to be discovered. On the shores of Jamaica Pond, at the Boston Alzheimer's Center, my father received the compassion and gentle care for which Boston's medical community is renowned. Near that pond, I was blessed to meet Rev. Ray Hammond, cofounder of the Ten Point Coalition, a devoted son whose mother lived adjacent to my father, and from whom I learned so much about the human spirit.

Boston is a kaleidoscope, and we just turn it to find another wonder. For me, one unforgettable discovery came the night I was introduced to the Boston Public Library. At a dinner in Bates Hall for the esteemed and inestimable John Kenneth Galbraith, I was captured by the rightness of the setting. Where else to honor a man of letters but in the nation's first public library? Do not merely walk by this building. Go in.

Meanwhile, enjoy this graceful book, and find your secret place. Be an explorer. Delve into Boston's nooks and crevices, and you'll flower, too.

—ROBIN BROWN
Boston hotelier

A City and Its Roots

Any tour guide can glide you by Boston and its environs. Point out the lyrical bandbox on Yawkey Way where John Updike and the Fenway faithful bid The Kid adieu. The Freedom Trail. The swan boats. The hillside from which colonial artillery once scared the Redcoats away. A swath of Southie captured in *Good Will Hunting*. The neighborhoods in Roxbury and Dorchester where Donna Summer or *Boston Boy* writer Nat Hentoff grew up. The downtown hotel known for its Parker House Rolls, less so for former employees Malcolm X and Ho Chi Minh.

But who will take you inside a nuclear reactor on a quiet street near Kendall Square? Lead you inside the clock tower you'd seen on old episodes of *Ally McBeal*? Take you on a heart-stopping ride in a Statie's souped-up Corvette? Who will venture into secret Masonic gatherings, or step gingerly toward underground train stations abandoned for generations?

These "Secret Spaces" represent places we locals might like to explore ourselves—if we didn't have to trudge to work, or do family chores, or complain about the commute or the weather. We hope the fifty sites selected here, chosen from more than a year's worth of persistent investigation, capture your imagination—and help reawaken a sense of adventure for this City on a Hill.

This book is the inspiration and reflection of the insatiable curiosity of Christine Makris, travel editor of Boston.com, who directed an extraordinary collaboration between *The Boston Globe* and its Web site to plumb our town for its hidden riches. The first images and accompanying captions published online and in print created a sensation, addictive to local readers who, like many in this town, think they've seen and known it all.

Makris and *Globe* assistant photo editor Leanne Burden Seidel plunged forward, overseeing a team of photographers and online producers who yielded our town's treasures. *Globe* editor Marty Baron saw the potential for this project, which resulted in the first partnership in two decades between the *Globe* and its once–wholly owned book-publishing unit, Globe Pequot Press, now known as GPP.

Thanks are due here to Patricia Harris and to David Lyon, who took the many voices of our news project and crafted their singular—and graceful—voice to the final text; to Janice Page, the Globe's energetic book development editor; and to Mary Norris, an editorial director at GPP, who shepherded this book to completion.

The beauty of this work lies in its surprises. As the poet Martin Espada has said, "Invisible Boston is full of invisible people." In reading through *Secret Spaces*, you already are opening a shuttered door, drawing open the curtains of a window. Prepare to engage. And discover anew what makes Boston distinctive.

—DAVID BEARD
Editor, Boston.com

Inside Bob Kraft's Box
Gillette Stadium

When the guy owns the team, it's only reasonable to expect that he might also lay claim to the ultimate den. Forget about envying the dream male hidey-hole jammed with Barcaloungers, La-Z-Boys, and a gigantic projection TV. Those who are bereft of a season ticket to Foxborough might find it a swell place to watch the gridiron matchups. But it can't hold a candle to the posh surroundings where Robert K. Kraft cheers on his New England Patriots, the National Football League franchise he purchased in 1994. When the Pats outgrew their old home turf, Kraft built bigger and newer Gillette Stadium—and gave himself the best seats in the house. His personal skybox may be up among the nosebleed seats, but that just ensures his view is rivaled only by the blimp shots. And there's not a trace of Naugahyde in sight.

Kraft and his lucky skybox guests stretch out on custom-upholstered theater seats to watch the Patriots march down the field. When the big guys stop grunting and shoving each other for a few minutes so the network can go to commercial, Kraft and company can stroll over to the massive bar to get a drink.

Even the memorabilia enshrined in Kraft's working den trumps the pennants, posters, and other pigskin paraphernalia tacked up on the wood paneling of that Pats-obsessed neighbor down the street. How many guys can display the ball from the dramatic "Snow Game"—the 2001 divisional playoff victory over the Oakland Raiders that closed out Foxborough Stadium in style? Or the kickoff and first touchdown balls from the September 9, 2002, inaugural game at Gillette Stadium? Super Bowl trophies may belong to the fans, as Kraft always says, but prizes like those are reminders that the guy who owns the team is always on the ball.

For more information on Gillette Stadium in Foxborough, Massachusetts, visit www.gillettestadium.com.

Where Plants Propagate
Dana Greenhouse, Arnold Arboretum

"Great oaks from little acorns grow," or so the saying goes—but it's not always that easy. The plant propagators at Harvard University's Arnold Arboretum can't always trust nature to take its course. Maintaining the genetic integrity of one of the world's great botanical reference collections can't be left to the vagaries of open pollination. So, many of the stately trees and lush shrubs of the open-air living library of woody plants began their lives inside the Arboretum's Charles Stratton Dana Greenhouses.

The bequest that launched the arboretum in 1872 specified that it would "contain, as far as practicable, all the trees [and] shrubs . . . either indigenous or exotic, which can be raised in the open air." But that doesn't mean they can't get a head start. Think of the Dana Greenhouses, built in 1963, as the nursery, where it's always springtime and the moist air smells of rich humus.

Plant propagator Jack Alexander, who has worked at the Arboretum since the mid-1970s, spends his days planting and nurturing seeds, taking and rooting cuttings, and even growing specimens from laboratory tissue cultures to keep the 265-acre Jamaica Plain landscape stocked. "We're constantly growing, constantly replacing plants that may be in bad condition or dead," Alexander explains.

Maintaining more than 7,000 plants representing more than 4,500 named varietals is no small task, especially since every plant on the grounds has its own number and database entry. Over the years, the Arboretum has led the way in botanical and horticultural exploration around the world, especially in eastern Asia, and has introduced many of their explorers' finds to popular cultivation.

More than just a nursery, the Dana Greenhouses are also an ark. The seed herbarium within the greenhouses contains roughly 1,500 specimens of rare and unusual plants from around the globe.

The Arnold Arboretum is at 125 Arborway in Jamaica Plain. For more information visit www.arboretum .harvard.edu.

Checking into a "Haunted" Hotel
The Omni Parker House Hotel

His square face framed in a beard, Harvey D. Parker's portrait hangs in the dining room of the hotel he built in 1855. But there are those who say that Harvey, or at least his ectoplasm, still appears in person from time to time. Nor is the legendary hotelier the only spirit said to haunt the oldest continuously operating hotel in the country, the Omni Parker House Hotel. In his 1884 poem, "At the Breakfast Club," Oliver Wendell Holmes remarked on the phenomenon: "Such guests! What famous names its record boasts / Whose owners wander in the mob of ghosts!"

Intimations of the paranormal are sometimes subtle. The elevator keeps showing up on the third floor, even though no one calls it. Some say it's Charles Dickens, heading to bed in the Dickens Room, where he stayed in 1867 and 1868 during a reading tour. Others suggest that it is the spirit of tragic actress Charlotte Cushman, who died in the same room in 1876 (the only confirmed in-room death in the hotel's history). The mirror where Dickens stood to practice for his debut public reading of *A Christmas Carol* still hangs on the wall, but some observers say it fails to reflect certain objects.

The presiding spirit seems to be Parker himself. One guest reported seeing a man in nineteenth-century attire appear in Room 1012 and smile at her and her sleeping mother—then suddenly disappear. She was shocked to recognize the apparition when she saw Parker's portrait at breakfast. Stories abound of tenth-floor paranormal activities, notably raucous carryings-on of a mysterious man wearing a stovepipe hat and reeking of whiskey and cigars.

Staff and guests alike have also reported ghostly images flickering in the glass panel between the restaurant and the bar. Perhaps Harvey's heading for an after-dinner brandy.

The Omni Parker House Hotel is located at 60 School Street in downtown Boston. For more information visit www.omnihotels.com/FindAHotel/BostonParker House.aspx.

Beneath the Ether Dome
Massachusetts General Hospital

The fourth-floor operating theater in the oldest part of Massachusetts General Hospital is, one could say, a real knockout. Designed by Charles Bulfinch (architect of the State House) and constructed from drawings by Alexander Parris (architect of Quincy Market), the Bulfinch Pavilion is distinguished by the great glass dome that provided bright daylight to illuminate operations in the days before electricity. (The room was a surgical theater from 1823 to 1868.)

But the architectural pedigree is only part of the story. Events of October 16, 1846, immortalized the spot. Using a device of his own invention, dentist William Thomas Green Morton administered ether to patient Gilbert Abbot, knocking the poor man out so that Dr. John Warren could remove a tumor from Abbot's neck. It was the first widely announced demonstration of general anesthesia. Following the operation's success, Dr. Warren proclaimed, "We have conquered pain!" If Abbot had any comments, they were not recorded for posterity. Doctors quickly adopted ether as a surgical anesthetic, and the room became known as the Ether Dome.

It's still used for academic conferences and lectures, and houses a small museum of the history of anesthesiology. The complex of rooms beneath the dome also displays some peculiar objects from medical history, including a full skeleton once used to teach anatomy, and the dome's most famous resident: the 2,500-year-old Egyptian mummy of Theban stonecutter Padihershef, which was donated to the hospital in 1823 by Dutch merchant Jacob van Lennep. One of the first Egyptian mummies brought to the United States, Padihershef was unwrapped and examined at Mass General, then exhibited in Boston, New York, Charleston, Philadelphia, and Baltimore before returning to his permanent (more or less) home beneath the Ether Dome's panes.

The Ether Dome is located in the Bulfinch Pavilion at Massachusetts General Hospital at Cambridge and Fruit Streets in Boston. See www.massgeneral.org/vep for tour schedule.

Inspecting the Gilding
Massachusetts State House

The dome atop the State House has been its most iconic attribute since the building opened in January 1798 to take over the governmental functions of the Old State House, which was left standing. The view over Beacon Street from the top of the oldest large-domed public building in the country is equal parts inspirational and dizzying. From the time it opened until the advent of skyscrapers, the Massachusetts State House dominated the Boston skyline. It serves as the zero-mile marker for Massachusetts roads—providing some local justification for the hyperbolic 1858 assertion by Oliver Wendell Holmes that the State House was "the hub of the Solar System."

But the dome did not always shine like the sun. The original was covered in gray-painted shingles, leading legislators to fret over leaks and the possibility of fire. In 1802 they commissioned Paul Revere & Sons to sheathe the dome in copper to protect it against fire and water alike. In 1874 the dome was gilded with 23-karat gold leaf. When the dome was regilded in 1997, it cost $300,000—more than one hundred times the cost of the original job. According to Tammy Kraus, director of State House operations, six pounds of gold leaf, which is as thin as the cellophane wrapper on a package of cigarettes, was delivered in a shoebox.

The cupola that provides the privileged view over the dome for a lucky few is also a replacement. The new cupola installed in 1859 was a third larger than the original in Charles Bulfinch's design. But the builders left intact the pinecone that has functioned as a finial on the cupola from the outset. According to Kraus, it symbolizes the importance of the lumber industry to the early New England economy.

The Massachusetts State House is located atop Beacon Hill at the corner of Beacon and Park Streets in Boston. Tours are offered weekdays from 10:00 a.m. to 4:00 p.m. For more information visit www.sec.state.ma.us/trs.

Inside the Green Igloo
Boston Public Garden

Longfellow's village blacksmith may have stood tall beneath a spreading chestnut tree, but lovebirds and picnickers can lie low under the weeping European beech tree at the Boston Public Garden. There's something surprising about finding such a private space in such a public place, steps from the Swan Boats, a beechnut's toss from the footbridge. To recline beneath the tree (officially discouraged by Boston Parks & Recreation, by the way, to keep the grass from being trampled) is to hide in plain sight. The thick green

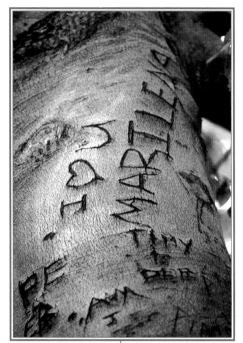

canopy of this specimen of *Fagus sylvatica* 'Pendula' runs true to form for the specially bred varietal, forming more of a capelike enclosure than a dome. It's open on the sidewalk side, yet as people and their dogs walk by, everyone watches the waters of the pond and no one seems to see the tree.

Recliners who remain statue-still in the dappled light that filters through the thick, broad leaves are invisible as they watch oblivious stroller-pushers and dog-leash holders. A water-

world drama plays out in full view from beneath the leaves as mallard ducks swoop in for splashy, quacky landings, and the swans cruise the pond's glassy surface like avian schooners. Soon they'll stop to feed, crossing necks as they dip down below the surface. They're hardly the only lovebirds in evidence, as the fading scars of initials, names, and hearts and arrows on the beech's trunk and branches overhead make clear. Its bower is hardly cloistered in some far corner of the Public Garden's twenty-four acres. The tree, estimated to be between fifty and eighty years old, stands between the footbridge and the dry fountain of the Triton Babies, unremarkable until it is inhabited.

The Boston Public Garden, located in the heart of downtown Boston, runs parallel to Boylston Street, between Arlington and Charles Streets. For more information on the Garden and its horticulture, visit www.friendsofthepublic garden.org.

Helping the Planes Land
Logan International Airport

Oh, the comings and goings! With direct flights to more than one hundred destinations around the globe, Logan International Airport is the busiest transport hub in New England and, acre for acre, one of the busiest airports in the world. The twenty-two-story, 285-foot-high control tower at Logan was the largest in the world when it was built in 1973, for $7.2 million. Providing both a recognizable landmark for pilots (the twin pylon construction is unique in the Northeast) and a comprehensive 360-degree view of

the airport, runways, and surrounding airspace, it is truly the all-seeing eye above Boston.

Although the East Boston field is physically one of the nation's smallest high-traffic airports, Federal Aviation Administration air traffic controllers still have to keep their eyes on six runways, 14 miles of taxiways, and 237 acres of concrete and asphalt apron. Look both ways before crossing the street? That's just for starters—in the air, it's essential to look up, down, forward, and backward as well.

Until 2001, visitors could take in the views from a sixteenth-floor observation deck and perhaps appreciate a little of the skill that the traffic cops of the sky exercise in keeping Logan moving smoothly. (It's now closed for security reasons.) Here, from left to right, controllers Charlie Milan, Matt McCluskey, and John Melecio clear planes for takeoffs and landings. The team has its hands full—in 2006 Logan was the twenty-third busiest tower in the country, handling 415,073 takeoffs and landings, according to Arlene Salac-Murray, manager of the FAA's Office of External Communications. Its fifty-six scheduled and nonscheduled air carriers (including twenty-nine domestic and sixteen foreign-flag airlines) send nearly twenty-eight million travelers on their way, ranking Logan twentieth nationwide in passenger volume.

The Logan International Airport is located at 1 Harborside Drive in East Boston. For general information visit the Web site at www.massport.com/Logan.

Meeting the Lady in Black
Fort Warren, Georges Island

Was there ever a fort without a ghost? Or at least the story of a ghost? Even Fort Warren on Georges Island in Boston Harbor—which had a relatively peaceful history, as far as fortresses go—is said to be haunted by the Ghost of the Lady in

Black, wife of a Confederate soldier. Fort Warren was finished just before the outbreak of the Civil War. While no Rebel ships ever assailed its bastions, it did serve as a prison camp for captured Confederate soldiers, sailors, and politicians.

The ghost story seems to have originated with historian and popular tale-teller Edward Rowe Snow, "without the slightest guarantee that any part of it is true." In his account, a Georgia woman dressed as a man to break into the fort to help her husband escape. Caught by guards, she was sentenced to death as a spy. To accommodate her final request to die in women's clothes, she was hanged in black robes that had been used in a play the soldiers put on for entertainment.

Snow told tales of spooky appearances of the Ghost of the Lady in Black—leaving fresh prints in new-fallen snow that suddenly disappeared, warning a sergeant in the 1930s not to enter the part of the fort once used as a dungeon, and chasing one poor sentry from his post. Several men were court-martialed for firing shots at a ghostly apparition.

The light seen in this picture baffles *Boston Globe* photographer John Tlumacki. "I can't explain what the streaks of lights are in the pitch-black coal room tunnel where a group of kids from Lexington Christian Academy were passing through," he says. "One of them had a flashlight, but nobody passed through the tunnel during the two-second exposure."

Fort Warren is on Georges Island, one of the Boston Harbor Islands. For information on ferry service to the islands, visit www.bostonislands.org.

Lighting the Lanterns
Old North Church

It's an arduous climb up steep, narrow steps to the 191-foot-high steeple atop Old North Church. The original was placed on the 1723 church in 1740—making it the tallest point in Boston. In 1757 daredevil John Childs leapt from the steeple with a feathered glider lashed to his back and sailed safely along a rope tether to land some 700 feet away. His first demonstration drew such crowds that he performed the stunt twice more the next day, so upsetting normal business that Boston authorities barred him from repeat performances.

Childs's first known human flights in America might have marked the steeple's high points in history if not for the events of April 18, 1775. As every schoolchild knows, church sexton Robert Newman climbed to the top of the steeple to hang the two lanterns that told Paul Revere that the British were crossing the harbor by sea to march on Lexington and Concord rather than taking the longer land route. The rest, as they say, is history.

Although that steeple was toppled in the gale of 1804, Henry Wadsworth Longfellow climbed its replacement (twenty feet shorter) for inspiration before he wrote his poem, "The Midnight Ride of Paul Revere." When the replacement steeple blew down during Hurricane Carol in 1954, it was replaced with the exact replica of the original that still stands today. The twin lanterns in the window are lit by flipping a switch in the archives room, lower down in the steeple.

A descendent of Newman does the honors every year on the evening before Patriots Day. Otherwise, the lanterns are lit only for special occasions—sometimes somber (the deaths of Presidents Reagan and Ford), sometimes celebratory (recent Red Sox World Series and Patriots Super Bowl wins).

Old North Church is at 193 Salem Street, Boston. For information about tours visit www.oldnorth.org.

Where the Wild Things Are
Harvard Museum of Natural History

Most visitors to the Harvard Museum of Natural History make a beeline for the blooms, so to speak, marveling over the Glass Flowers. The kids often go straight to the mineralogical collection, where shiny geodes and mute meteorites set little eyes to gleaming. But down a labyrinth of corridors seemingly as tangled and branched as the evolutionary tree are case upon case of zoological specimens, many of which you wouldn't want to encounter in a dark jungle.

The reddish-green guenon, for example, is an impressively fanged little monkey found in eastern Africa. Unlike its arboreal cousins, this guenon scampers around on the ground in small troupes, giving him good reason to show some teeth when threatened. Guenons usually look much more peaceful. (Imagine this one's mother scolding him: "If you're not careful, your face will freeze like that!")

The Flying Fox might look like an extra from a Bela Lugosi movie, but the Philippine fruit bat is a strict vegetarian (it's hard to grow this big on a diet of mosquitoes). More than three hundred Philippine plant species—including bananas, mangoes, avocados, and cashews—depend on the fruit bats for pollination or seed dispersal.

On the other hand, no one will catch the growling Bengal tiger ordering a salad. This impressive beast is one of about five hundred large zoological specimens on display at the Harvard Museum of Natural History (there are more than twelve thousand items displayed, but that's counting the drawers of beetles). Some visitors find the scariest display to be the coastal gorillas mugging on tree limbs like a bunch of juvenile delinquents. The halls go on and on, hiding such treasures as a hippo, a giraffe, and one of the few taxidermied dodo birds in the world.

And lions and tigers and bears—oh my!

The Harvard Museum of Natural History is at 26 Oxford Street, Cambridge. For information on touring the museum, visit hmnh.harvard.edu.

Where Time Unwinds
The Old State House

In the early days of the Republic, Simon Willard was the guy you called on to get the right time in the most graceful way possible. Just as the fanciest church needed a Revere bell, the most prominent building in town needed a Willard clock. So when the Old State House, built in 1713, was turned into City Hall in 1830, the city fathers called on Simon Willard to build the timepiece. It was installed in 1831.

Over nearly nine score years, the clock has taken a licking (including removal between 1956 and 1976 in favor of a sundial), but it keeps on ticking. That's because someone (here, Old State House museum associate Denise Rubio) climbs up among the dusty scaffolding and charred beams under the roof to crank the mechanism that hoists the weights. Although Willard was known for popularizing the eight-day clock, this wasn't one of them. It has to be wound twice a week—usually on Monday and Friday—and the journey to the mechanism requires climbing nineteen steps from the first to the second floor, twenty-two more narrow and twisting steps from the second floor to the third, and sixteen tight steps from the third floor to the attic.

Willard's mechanism was a model of precision for 1831—especially considering its gears were all hand-filed—but it loses about five minutes between windings. The lucky soul designated as clock-setter must lean out a small window in the clock face on the east façade of the Old State House and pull the hands into place—often with direction from the crowds on State Street below. The clock-setter's recompense is the chance to see the mechanism up close. The clockwork features brass gears, a steel and iron framework, and a small brass finial on top. Willard built for the ages, measured one minute at a time.

The Old State House is at the corner of Washington and State Streets, Boston. For information visit www.boston history.org.

Where Brides Cry
Priscilla of Boston

Most young girls dream of looking like a princess when they walk down the aisle on their wedding day. But by the time young women arrive at Priscilla of Boston, "they have developed their own style," says Marie Donovan, manager of the flagship bridal salon on Boylston Street in Boston.

Each bride-to-be, who is usually accompanied by her posse of mother and attendants, gets a large private dressing room and the assistance of a personal consultant to help with the excruciating decision. After she provides details on her wedding venue and personal style preferences, the typical customer tries on from eight to ten gowns before finding the right dress. "We can tell when everyone starts crying," says Donovan, "and we have to go around with tissues."

Priscilla Kidder opened her first shop on Newbury Street in 1945 to outfit the rush of postwar brides. Fashion historians often point to her as the woman who took the simple white dress and embellished it with intricate bead- and lacework. In the process, she expanded the concept of the wedding gown into a couture statement as special as the occasion.

To help brides better appreciate the details of the gowns they try on, the main salon has mirrors on all four walls and dimmer switches so that the lighting can better approximate the wedding setting. It can take up to nine months from gown selection to final fitting, making January to March the busiest months in the salon. This shop set a sales record in 2007, when it sent about 2,500 brides (including Shauna Antley, seen here with sales assistant Carolyn Dumser) down the aisles in dresses that exceeded their girlish dreams.

Priscilla of Boston is at 801 Boylston Street, Boston. For more information visit www.priscillaofboston.com.

In the Eye of the Storm
The National Weather Service

There's an old saying that if you don't like the weather in New England, wait five minutes and it will change. The National Weather Service (NWS) office in Taunton—the hub of weather forecasts, warnings, and advisories for most of Massachusetts, Rhode Island, northern Connecticut, and parts of southern New Hampshire—takes that changeable atmosphere in stride. No one minds the forecast of high pressure and sunny skies, but if high winds, a thunderstorm, flash flood, tornado, coastal flood, severe snow, or ice storm is on the way, the Taunton staff issues the appropriate warnings and weather advisories.

While many of his fellow meteorologists get visibly excited by the prospects of a blizzard, "I find summer weather to be fascinating," says Bill Babcock, seen here going over information with meteorologist Eleanor Vallier-Talbot. "The scope of weather—the idea of something developing, and to understand why—is what I find fascinating." The screens in the foreground of the photo are part of the Advanced Weather Information Processing System.

The office, built in 1993, was located in Taunton because it's equidistant between Boston and Providence, giving the Doppler radar excellent coverage of both metropolitan districts. In addition to forecasts for thirty-five land-based zones, the NWS Taunton office issues marine forecasts, warnings, and advisories for the coastal waters from the Merrimack River, Massachusetts, to Watch Hill, Rhode Island. It also provides weather information to Logan International Airport and seven other southern New England airports.

As the nerve center for a range of critical public services, the office discontinued public tours after September 11, 2001. But "there's not a day that this office is closed," says Babcock. Even before clouds threaten on the horizon, the staff in Taunton knows which way the wind blows.

For more information on location, weather updates, and general information, visit the center's Web site at www.erh.noaa.gov.

To the Center of the Earth
The Mapparium at the Mary Baker Eddy Library

Visitors standing on the bridge that cuts through the Mapparium at the Mary Baker Eddy Library at the Christian Science Center in Back Bay generally have no idea that the three-story-high glass structure is "like a balloon on a stand," according to M. J. Pullins, the library's marketing manager. "It's truly a round room made of glass, enclosed in a boxlike room."

But there's a secret space that's literally out of this world. Library staff members occasionally get the Atlas-eye's view of the planet when they move items in and out of the storage area beneath the Mapparium. But they definitely have to observe the librarian's code of silence (*SHHHHHHH!!!*) when they enter or leave the space since any sounds can be heard inside the globe. (Sound travels so well inside the Mapparium that people at opposite ends of the thirty-foot walkway can converse by whispering to each other.)

Construction of the Mapparium—608 curved stained-glass panels set in a bronze framework—began in April 1934 and was finished in June 1935. Artists for Rand McNally in Chicago used their 1934 world map to draw the paper cartoons that served as templates for the glass panels. The political boundaries have remained fixed ever since. Committees discussed updating them in 1939, 1958, and 1966, but each time concluded that the Mapparium was more important as a work of art than as a geopolitical reference. During a 1998–2002 renovation, workers cleaned and repaired the glass and installed a state-of-the-art lighting and sound system.

A bottom hatch—at the South Pole—is opened about once a month to clean out objects (usually paper admission stickers) that fall to the bottom of the world. Staff members discourage visitors from dropping coins, which could damage the glass. No cell phones or water bottles are allowed on the journey through the center of the earth.

The Mapparium is located at the Mary Baker Eddy Library, 200 Massachusetts Avenue, Boston, between Huntington Avenue and Boylston Street. For more information visit www.marybakereddylibrary.org.

Sleeping at a Crime Scene
Lizzie Borden Bed & Breakfast

Of the eight Victorian-style guest rooms at the Lizzie Borden Bed & Breakfast at 92 Second Street in Fall River, the most popular are the Lizzie Borden Room and the John V. Morse Room, where Abby D. Borden's body was discovered on the morning of August 4, 1892. Abby and her husband, Andrew Borden, had been brutally bludgeoned to death, with wounds consistent with a hatchet attack. Thirty-two-year-old Lizzie Borden was accused and tried for the murders of her father and stepmother. At the end of the lurid thirteen-day trial, the jury deliberated just one hour before returning a verdict of "not guilty." No one else was ever arrested or charged with the murders, and Borden lived out her life in another Fall River house.

Fascination with the case continues. According to B&B co-owner Lee-ann Wilbur, most guests are drawn to the property by its history as the site of the "crime of the century." A group of mystery writers books the entire B&B each year on the Sunday nearest Lizzie's July 19 birthday, and demand for the Morse room on the anniversary of the murders is so great that the B&B auctions it on eBay. But wherever guests sleep, they can lounge in the parlor where Andrew's body was found. Wilbur is convinced that she can sense the presence of the paterfamilias in the house. "It's his house—he's not going anywhere," she says, adding that the spirit used to blow out lightbulbs but now merely throws circuit breakers.

But Wilbur refuses to be spooked. "I just have fun with it," she says. "If I really thought about it, I couldn't stay here." When potential guests who are simply looking for a nice Victorian B&B call, she asks, "Do you know what happened here?"

For more information on the Lizzie Borden Bed & Breakfast, visit www.lizzie-borden.com.

Looking through Tom Brady's Locker
Gillette Stadium

It's a safe bet that most sports reporters took little notice when the Patriots selected the University of Michigan quarterback as the 199th pick in the National Football League draft of 2000. Nor did they swarm all over the fourth-string quarterback in his rookie season, even though Tom Brady did advance to the number-two spot

behind Drew Bledsoe by season's end. After all, he saw limited playing time and completed exactly one pass in three attempts. Then Bledsoe's injury in September 2001 thrust Brady into the spotlight. By the end of the year, Brady was crowned the MVP of Super Bowl XXXVI. The rest is destiny.

So now the crowd gets there early on Wednesday during football season, vying for a spot at Tom Brady's Gillette Stadium locker, where the Patriots quarterback is always greeted by a horde of reporters awaiting his weekly availability. "Camera operators stand on stools in a crowd that can run ten layers deep," said *Boston Globe* Patriots beat writer Mike Reiss, while "print reporters reach in with their recorders to get close enough to hear what Brady is saying." Those who get there late find themselves trying to eavesdrop from the outer wall of reporters.

When Patriots quarterback Tom Brady isn't there (as during most of the 2008 season, when he was sidelined with knee injuries), neither is the crowd of media members usually perched around his space. His locker looks little different from the rest of his teammates' personal spaces in the cavernous locker room at Gillette Stadium—including those of recent neighbors such as Randy Moss and Jabar Gaffney. Few personal items, besides a pair of jeans, hint that New England's biggest sports star calls this locker his own.

For more information on Gillette Stadium and the New England Patriots, visit www.gillettestadium.com.

Hanging Out over Fenway
The Hood America A-60 Plus Lightship

There's something about a dirigible, especially when it's lit from inside at night, that puts a smile on people's faces. Here, pilot Katharine Board sits at the controls of the Hood blimp en route from the Beverly airport to Boston, where it will assume its familiar position hovering over Fenway Park. The Hood Blimp (technically, the Hood America A-60 Plus Lightship) is one of fewer than a dozen dirigibles around the world equipped with high-definition video cameras to serve as an aerial observation platform. It's not floating above Fenway Park just to make the fans feel good about Hood—it's up there to provide a video feed to the New England Sports Network.

The blimp might sound like a great place to view the game—except that there's no bathroom in the cabin, which is attached to a 128-foot-long balloon puffed up with 68,000 cubic feet of helium. Technically, there's room onboard for two pilots and up to three passengers, but with the gyroscopically stabilized high-def cameras in place, there's barely room for a photographer.

The blimp cruises at thirty-two miles per hour and tops out at a speed-limit-friendly fifty-five miles per hour. But Board doesn't sweat getting to the game on time, since there isn't a lot of traffic where she's flying. With a fuel consumption of four gallons per hour at cruising speed, this floating billboard powered by twin eighty-horsepower engines probably gets better mileage than some sport utility vehicles stuck in rush-hour traffic trying to get to the game.

In addition to Fenway, the blimp also flies over some other baseball parks for Pawtucket Red Sox, Lowell Spinners, and Portland Seadogs games. The friendly airship also hovers above other mass events, like the Yarmouth (Maine) Clam Festival and the Boston Pops Independence Day concert on the Esplanade.

For more information on the Hood blimp, visit Hood's Web site at www.hphood.com.

Training Puppies in Prison
Northeastern Correctional Center

Peter Hilliard and Morgan, a black Labrador retriever puppy, might look like the archetype of a man and his dog, but their interaction is serious business. Hilliard is an inmate at Northeastern Correctional Center in Concord, and Morgan is enrolled in the Prison Puppy program of NEADS/ Dogs for Deaf and Disabled Americans. (NEADS stands for National Education for Assistance Dogs Services.) Inmates selected for the program make a commitment of up to two years to train a puppy as a service dog to assist people with disabilities. Inmate trainer and puppy live together around the clock, which means the pup also interacts with other inmates and staff at the facility. "They go along with the inmate to programs, classes, recreation areas, medical appointments, the visiting room, and chow halls for meals," explains Department of Corrections spokesperson Diane Wiffin. "If the inmate also holds an institutional job, a backup inmate handler is available."

As service dogs in training, the pups learn basic obedience and such tasks as operating light

switches, opening doors, fetching objects, helping put on or take off socks, and accompanying a wheelchair. According to Sheila O'Brien, executive director of NEADS, the majority of the animals trained as service dogs are Labrador retrievers because they are eager to please and are such good retrievers.

"It's a win-win situation," says O'Brien. "The inmate learns to nurture and to have responsibility for another living creature. And with the inmates' hard work, we've gone from a four-year wait for service dogs down to about a year and a half. We're starting to place dogs now with veterans from the Iraq war."

Sometimes trainer and dog are reunited. "If a client wants to meet the inmate handler," O'Brien says, "we'll often bring the dog back for a visit. It's something to see—they never forget who raised them as puppies."

For inquiries relating to the training program or the Northeastern Correctional Center, call (978) 371-7941, or visit www.mass.gov.

Inside the Green Monster
Fenway Park

There's plenty of electronic pizzazz around Fenway Park with the giant centerfield electronic board and other monitors on the left- and right-field lines that chart hits, runs, and errors and remind spectators who's on the mound. But the official scoreboard is embedded in the Green Monster. It's one of the last manual scoreboards in a Major League Baseball park (others are at Chicago's Wrigley Field and Seattle's Safeco Field). There are a few concessions to automation, like the red and green lights to indicate strikes, balls, and outs. But the official record of the game is hung manually.

Christian Elias (opposite, top and bottom right) has been the Red Sox scorekeeper for nearly two decades, while Nate Moulter (bottom left) signed on as an assistant more recently. On the walls inside the scoreboard are signatures of some of the Sox players from over the years—and a few of their opponents. (Before he traded his Red Sox uniform for Dodger blue, left fielder Manny Ramirez was known to pop in frequently.) Look closely on the vertical strips on the front of the scoreboard and you will spy the initials TAY and JRY—for former team owners Thomas Austin Yawkey and Jean Remington Yawkey—in Morse code.

Hanging the score by hand is part of "the old mystique of the tradition of Fenway. It's a reminder of the illustrious history of the Red Sox," says Marty Ray of the Red Sox public relations staff. "It's a generational connect. You know when you're watching the game it's being scored the same way your grandfather watched it scored."

As the Tim Robbins character in *Bull Durham* quipped, "A good friend of mine used to say, 'This is a very simple game. You throw the ball, you catch the ball, you hit the ball. Sometimes you win, sometimes you lose, sometimes it rains.'"

Thus it has ever been. At Fenway, it still is.

Fenway Park is at 4 Yawkey Way, Boston. For information on park tours, visit www.redsox.com.

Making Your Own Electrical Storm
The Van de Graaff Generator at the Museum of Science

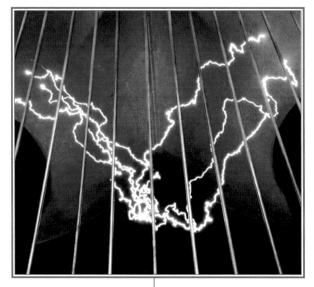

It doesn't take Zeus to throw a lightning bolt—at least not at the Museum of Science, where education associates like Daniel A. Davis, shown here, do it twice a day and three times on Friday in the Thomson Theatre of Electricity.

They simply crank up the venerable Van de Graaff generator, a device first developed in 1929 by physicist Robert Jemison Van de Graaff. The Museum of Science's model is the world's largest air-insulated generator and was built by Van de Graaff himself. It was originally used at the Massachusetts Institute of Technology as a research tool in early atom-smashing and high-energy X-ray experiments and was donated to the museum in 1959.

The device works by using a rotating belt to separate positive and negative charges by friction—not unlike rubbing a latex balloon on your hair to build up a static charge—and transferring the charge to the surface of a metal dome.

This particular generator can build up a charge of 2.5 million volts, resulting in sparks that can jump as much as 15 feet—indoor lightning! During such demonstrations, no one goes inside the metal dome, where Davis is pictured.

Despite the high voltages, the current is small and the spectacular demonstrations are completely safe. During one phase of the demonstration, a presenter enters a metal cage that is raised into range—where it is struck by a giant spark. But, says Museum of Science spokesperson Mike Morrison, the intrepid demonstrator doesn't even end up with a bad hair day.

The Museum of Science is located at Science Park atop the Charles River Dam between Boston and Cambridge. For more information visit www.mos.org.

Bridging the Gender Gap
Jacque's Cabaret

Located just outside the Theater District in residential Bay Village, Jacque's exhorts its patrons to keep down the noise on the street out of respect for the neighbors. That might sound a little prim for a raucous bar, but the live-and-let-live stance has kept the doors open on the drag queen cabaret for more than a quarter century. And there's plenty of frivolity inside, with shows seven nights a week, every day of the year.

Mizery, pictured here, is a drag queen known for her dancing and signature makeup, which she can apply in a relative flash (fifteen minutes or so). She has been mixing masculinity and femininity professionally to the delight of Jacque's audiences for more than a decade.

"I don't have a problem distinguishing myself onstage and offstage. Other people have a problem with that. They either want you as a girl or they want you as a boy. There's no in-between, so it's so tough," she said in a recent documentary of her life, *Mizery*, by Carmen Oquendo-Villar.

Mizery and fellow longtime Jacque's performer Kris Knievil (opposite page, bottom) are among the few regulars who have their own dressing rooms at the club where they can store some of their wardrobe. (Some performers have entire apartments stuffed with costumes.)

On weeknights, when the entertainment can range from karaoke to stand-up to skits, Jacque's usually features three to four performers. As many as five drag queens take the stage on weekends, when the place is packed. Some Saturday nights, the performers may be the only men (technically) in the place, as Jacque's is an especially popular venue for bachelorette parties where, well, girls can be girls, and the only guys around can strut and kick like Rockettes.

Jacque's can be found at 79 Broadway, Boston. For more information visit www.jacquescabaret.com.

Swimming with the Sharks
New England Aquarium

Several times a day, staff divers for the New England Aquarium get in the swim of things, so to speak, when they join the sea turtles, barracudas, sand tiger sharks, stingrays, moray eels, and vibrant reef fish in their watery world. In all, about 600 creatures inhabit the aquarium's 200,000-gallon Giant Ocean Tank, where the 74-degree water and handmade artificial coral add a touch of the Caribbean to Boston's waterfront.

Not only do the divers have to clean the tank and regularly monitor water quality, they also have to feed the hungry denizens twice a day. The tank residents eat about fifteen pounds of food a day, including fish, squid, shrimp, and even such produce as corn, lettuce, and other greens. As you can imagine, the diver is very popular at feeding time. Dive safety officer John Hanzi is approached by sharks in the tank and even feeds shrimp directly into the mouth of a stingray. He says he is particularly fond of Myrtle, a giant green sea turtle, who likes him to scratch her shell with a conch shell.

Myrtle is also a favorite with visitors who follow the winding pathway around the four-story tank. She's been at the aquarium since it opened in 1969, charming children and adults alike. Her favorite food is brussels sprouts, though she also grazes on red peppers, broccoli, and cauliflower. Squid, shrimp, and pollock provide protein.

In addition to the aquarium's five permanent divers, several students and interns and about a dozen volunteer divers also get the rare opportunity to swim with the fishes.

The New England Aquarium is located at Central Wharf. For more information visit www.neaq.org.

Working for a Scoop
Breyers Ice Cream Plant

The process of making ice cream has come a long way since William A. Breyer began hand-cranking his own cool concoction back in 1866. His product was so popular that the Philadelphia-based family opened its first wholesale manufacturing plant thirty years later. By 1918 the company was churning out more than one million gallons of ice cream a year. (Originally distributed only in the Northeast and Mid-Atlantic states, Breyers went national in 1984.) Today, this Breyers manufacturing facility in Framingham alone produces about 700,000 gallons a week to be shipped up and down the East Coast. The company's biggest markets? New York, Philadelphia, and Boston.

As shown here, the ice-cream flavor Bubble Yum goes through the extruding process as boxes spin along the production line. The ice cream is then cut on top to ensure that each box contains the proper amount.

The facility concentrates on Breyers All Natural Ice Cream, which has thirty flavors. But it also churns out such gooey contemporary favorites as Snickers, Oreo, and Peanut Butter Cup and the aforementioned Bubble Yum in the "Fun and Indulgent" line. The Framingham plant is also the only Breyers facility to make lactose-free ice cream as well as the classic checkerboard pattern of alternating squares of vanilla and chocolate ice creams, sold as "NASCAR Checkered Flag."

About 165 employees work in production and another 35 in plant maintenance. They are all welcome to take part in the daily ritual of ice cream tasting in the company's quality control lab.

Yum. Now that's a perk.

Visit the Breyers Web site at www.breyers.com for more information about their products and the way they are made.

Preparing Potions

The Cat, The Crow, and The Crown

Laurie Cabot has been practicing witchcraft for more than forty years, having learned the ins and outs of the ancient ways from English witches. The "Official Witch of Salem" runs her own shop, The Cat, The Crow, and The Crown on Pickering Wharf, where she installed a potion bar in the summer of 2008. The potions, she explains, are made with essential and scented oils infused with such materials as rowan leaves, stones, and sea salt. "They're proprietary potions," she says, "not secret formulas, but I don't share them. They represent a lot of years of knowledge." In fact, she wrote fifty-eight new formulas for the potion bar.

Witches can't afford secrecy. "Secrecy is very dangerous. If you do not define yourself, then others will define you," Cabot says. "That's what happened during the persecutions and the burning times. The only secrets we witches keep are personal—our feelings. They're not secret because they're dark, but because they are private."

In fact, Cabot has been indefatigable in her campaign for the acceptance of witchcraft as an art, science, and religion. "We have our Book of Shadows, where we kept our ways secret during the burning times," she says, "but we hope that witches never hide again."

The new potion bar at her shop is designed to streamline the process of ministering to individuals by making selected potions "that take into account their astrological energies and their needs," she says.

Here Cabot mixes a love potion that she made by combining rose and ambergris oils, then charging the blend "with magic." Explaining her choices of oils, Cabot explains that "they both have the components to attract love." Her potions can have different purposes, she says, but often deal with issues of love or money.

The Cat, The Crow, and The Crown is located at 63R Pickering Wharf, Salem. For more information visit www.lauriecabot.com.

IN MEMORIAM
SENIOR SCULLERS
WHO GAVE THEIR LIVES
IN WORLD WAR II

JOHN RADFORD ABBOT, JR.   '43
HENRY FORBES BIGELOW, JR.   '44
ARTHUR S. BROWN-SERMAN   '44
DAVID LORING   '45

Skulking amid the Sculls
Weld Boathouse

An unmistakable landmark along the Charles River, Harvard University's Weld Boathouse is steeped in the history of rowing on the Charles River and at Harvard. It was constructed in 1906, shortly after the death of George Walker Weld, whose obituary called him "the greatest benefactor Harvard ever had in rowing." In 1889 the lifelong bachelor scion of the Massachusetts Welds (distant cousin to former Massachusetts governor William Weld, who came from the New York branch) funded the first boathouse on this spot, which was moved upstream to make way for the current facility. The Weld Boathouse is now the oldest original boathouse on the Charles and over the last century-plus has never missed a season, according to Liz O'Leary, head coach of women's rowing at Harvard. It is the official home of Radcliffe Crew and intramural crews, and it serves as the university's center for instruction in recreational and competitive sculling.

About one hundred sweep and sculling hulls are stored in Weld. The rowing season starts as soon as the ice clears from the Charles River (usually in March) and continues into December. The busiest season is spring, when roughly five hundred students participate in six weeks of intramural rowing competitions. That's not counting the one hundred athletes on Harvard's varsity women's rowing team, known as Radcliffe Crew. (The women voted to keep the Radcliffe name when sports programs were merged in 1972.) On a given day, O'Leary says, another twenty to one hundred recreational scullers use the boats, but after 5:00 p.m., varsity athletes have priority.

The facility—which is available to all Harvard students, faculty, staff, and even alumni with an activities card—opens at 6:00 a.m. When those first rowers hit the river, the surface is often like glass. The sculls cut perfect Vs with their wakes in the misty dawn.

The Weld Boathouse is located along the Charles River off Massachusetts Avenue in Cambridge. For more information visit www.fas.harvard.edu/~weldbh/.

Building a Mystery
The Massachusetts Grand Lodge

Few organizations are more steeped in mystery than the Freemasons. Traces of the world's oldest fraternity, begun as a trade organization for freestone carvers, date from 1390. By the early eighteenth century, the Freemasons had become a gentleman's fraternity, but references to their craftsman roots endure in the Grand Lodge of Massachusetts on Tremont Street in Boston. The square and compass depicted in a mural remind members to "square" their actions by the square of virtue and to circumscribe their passions with a symbolic compass. The G in the center represents God and geometry.

The first Masonic lodge in the western hemisphere was founded in 1733 in Boston at a tavern near Faneuil Hall. In top left photo, left to right, Mason W. Russell, deputy grand master, and Roger W. Pageau, grand master, both of the Grand Lodge of Massachusetts, and Eugene A. Capobianco, past master of St. John Lodge, help commemorate the 275th anniversary of St. John Lodge in Boston, the oldest Freemason group in the United States.

Another early Masonic haunt was the still-extant Green Dragon Tavern, where Mason Paul Revere tossed back some pints. Today, there's about one Masonic Lodge for every two towns in Massachusetts. The Grand Lodge of Massachusetts, the third oldest in the world, serves as a governing body.

To join a fraternity that has included Voltaire, Mozart, Ben Franklin, Thurgood Marshall, and "Buzz" Aldrin, you must be an adult male who believes in a higher power. Specific religious affiliation is unimportant. "You need to believe in the idea that there is something greater," says Robert Huke, spokesman for the Massachusetts Grand Lodge. How members rise in rank and the associated rituals remain shrouded in mystery, as members are pledged to silence. Moreover, says Huke, "members cannot talk about the 'modes and methods of recognition,'" signs that Masons use to recognize one another.

The Massachusetts Grand Lodge of Masons is located at 186 Tremont Street in downtown Boston. For more information visit www.massfreemasonry.org.

Finding Respite
Bigelow Chapel, Mount Auburn Cemetery

They build for the ages at Mount Auburn Cemetery in Cambridge, America's first garden cemetery, consecrated in 1831. Only a decade after the Gothic Revival-style Bigelow Chapel was constructed of Quincy granite and opened in 1846, it was disassembled and rebuilt even stronger. But they got the stained-glass windows right the first time. Dr. Jacob Bigelow, a Harvard professor, second president of the cemetery, and designer of the chapel later named for

him, commissioned the rose and chancel windows from Ballantine & Allan in Edinburgh, Scotland. The luminous hand-painted windows are among Boston's earliest examples of the art form. They were carefully removed from the first building and reinstalled in its more sturdy replacement. Over the decades, many a mourner has sought comfort in the chancel window's image of a winged woman ascending to heaven with infants in her arms.

Most visitors discover the chapel as they stroll the National Historic Landmark cemetery to study the monuments, inspect the plantings, or pay respects to some of the notable figures who rest here—including architect Charles Bulfinch, poet Henry Wadsworth Longfellow, and museum founder Isabella Stewart Gardner. With fourteen pinnacles reaching toward heaven, the chapel is hard to miss. Though it is still used for memorial services and other events, the doors are usually locked, and visitors must content themselves with admiring the stained glass from the outside or peeking through small windows in the heavy wooden doors to get glimpses of the interior.

At the end of the nineteenth century, Mount Auburn's first crematorium was installed in the basement of Bigelow Chapel, and the chapel is the final resting place for the ashes of Wallace Clement Sabine (the father of architectural acoustics), Alexander Orlov (former KGB agent), and several other scientists and inventors.

Mount Auburn Cemetery is located at 580 Mount Auburn Street, Cambridge. For more information, visit www .mountauburn.org.

Beneath the Tobin Bridge
Massport Bridge Administration

The Massport staff members who oversee the Tobin Bridge have a unique perspective on the historic structure, which opened in 1950. Their offices, which they reach by ascending in an elevator from a parking lot on Rutherford Street, are tucked up under the tollbooths amid the bridge's steel support girders. So camouflaged are the offices that most people have never noticed them.

Massport Bridge Administration manager Kathy Glowik and four other staffers are responsible for purchasing, record-keeping, and auditing the toll collections. They work to the soundtrack of a steady rumble of traffic overhead. "In my office the bobblehead figure is always bobbling," Glowik says. The staff takes it all in stride, but vibrations in the offices caused by trucks passing overhead sometimes make visitors uneasy.

In addition to offices, the little structure with amazing views holds a kitchen and a break room for toll officers, who work around the clock. About 76,000 vehicles use the bridge every day to cross the Mystic River between Charlestown and Chelsea. Although the Tobin's sturdy green cantilevered trusses may have been upstaged in the glamour department by the soaring cables of the Leonard Zakim Bunker Hill Bridge, dedicated in 2002, the Tobin still holds the title of longest bridge in New England. At two and one quarter miles in length, it's a half mile longer than the Golden Gate Bridge and almost twice as long as the Brooklyn Bridge.

To learn more about the Tobin Bridge, visit www.massport .com/bridges/about.asp.

Working the Barre
The Boston Ballet

In an effort to make it look, well, effortless, dancers with the Boston Ballet spend as many as seven hours a day in practice. During the weeks when they are not performing, a typical day begins with company class at 9:45 in the morning. Often taught by artistic associate Trinidad Vives, the company class is designed to build skill, technique, and flexibility for the day ahead, according to Boston Ballet spokeswoman Jo Cardin. Dancers like Heather Waymack spend forty-five minutes doing barre work and warming up. During another forty-five minutes devoted to "center work," dancers start with slow movements that build in intensity, speed, and difficulty.

Founded by E. Virginia Williams in 1963, the Boston Ballet was the first professional repertory ballet company in New England. Over the years, the company has received national and international acclaim and toured widely. But home is a five-story redbrick headquarters building in the historic South End. Opened in 1991, the 60,000-square-foot building designed by architect Graham Gund features some of the largest and best-equipped dance studios in the country. It's part of the Boston Center for the Arts, a visual and performing arts complex that's a hub of activity and creative energy.

Dancers need that energy and inspiration to stay focused for the long day of work. Rehearsals run daily from 11:30 a.m. to 5:30 p.m. During the fifteen-minute break between company class and rehearsal, dancers like Katherine Hartsell get a chance to relax and remove their shoes. Hartsell has been with the company since 2004 and joined the corps de ballet in 2007. "Being a dancer is a full-time body-and-soul kind of job," she says. "There is much challenge in that intensity, but also much reward. This environment is infused with so much talent, and I am constantly learning about technique, artistry, and humanity by being immersed in it."

For information on the Boston Ballet season, visit www .bostonballet.org.

Basking in the Glow
The Citgo Sign

Bustling Kenmore Square just wouldn't look the same without the Citgo sign that punctuates the area from the roof of a Boston University building.

Bostonians and vistors alike rely on the sixty-by-sixty-foot piece of illuminated advertising art as a directional landmark. Let's face it —the flashing bands of red, white, and blue are hard to miss. Baseball fans tied to their television screens look forward to getting a glimpse of the sign whenever a batter whacks a home run over the left field wall of Fenway Park.

But few people ever get as close as the photographer who took these dramatic sunset shots from the top of 660 Beacon Street.

The sign was erected in 1965 and soon transcended its narrow purpose as an amusing billboard. It was heralded as a playful and dynamic piece of op art, perfectly in tune with the times. Preservationists and other sign supporters raised such an uproar in 1983 that Citgo abandoned plans to remove what might be its most famous piece of advertising. The sign has also survived five hurricanes and weathered a political storm in September 2006 when Boston City Council member Jerry P. McDermott demanded that it be removed after Venezuelan president Hugo Chavez called President George W. Bush "the devil." (Citgo is a subsidiary of Venezuela's state-owned oil company.)

But the local icon continues to cast its steady glow. In 2005 its roughly 6,000 neon tubes and 250 high-voltage transformers were replaced with more energy-efficient light-emitting diodes, which are controlled by computer.

Now that's surely a sign of the times.

The Citgo sign stands above Beacon Street in Kenmore Square.

Composing the Roar of
the Greasepaint
Blue Man Group

While most audience members find it hard to take their eyes off the Blue Men and their journeys of onstage experimentation, there's a surprise lurking on the loft about ten feet above the stage. That's where three musicians dabbed in glowing face paint like tribal markings produce the evening soundtrack.

"They are a part of this tribal, communal experience that the Blue Men want us all to have, and therefore dress the part," says Blue Man Group spokeswoman Joanne Barrett. "They are like shamans, supporting us on the 'quest' of the evening—plus, they just know how to rock."

Hari Hassin, resident music director of Blue Man Group Boston (the show debuted here in 1995), says the raised loft also separates the musicians in terms of consciousness. "The band is from the same kind of place as the Blue Men, but we are beyond experimentation. We're kind of like the three wise men—been there, done that."

The Blue Men always make up with the same greasepaint, a custom formulation called "Blue Man blue," while the musicians have a little more leeway in applying their multiple colors of glow paint, all made in-house from a secret recipe of which Hassin reveals only that it contains "all organic material." Prepping for a show, he says, takes about thirty minutes. "Our costumes are always the same."

Here Christina (opposite page, top) plays the zither while Michael Petrucci (behind her and above) handles the drums. "More often than not," Hassin says, "the audience usually thinks we're a video until, upon closer inspection, they figure out that we're real."

Or to paraphrase a famous frog, it's not easy being blue.

Blue Man Group performs at the Charles Playhouse, 74 Warrenton Street, Boston. For more information visit www.blueman.com.

Learning from Patient Patients
Brigham and Women's Hospital

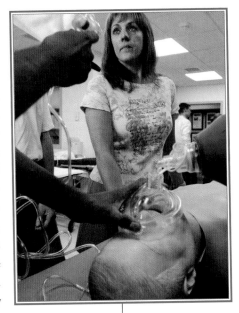

Students at the STRATUS Center at Brigham and Women's Hospital are no dummies—but some of their "patients" are. Launched in June 2004, the Simulation Training Research and Technology Utilization System Center has already helped to train more than five thousand doctors, nurses, emergency medical technicians, and even surgeons in courses that can range from a single hour to as long as three days. The "dummies" are actually simulators—complete with heartbeats, breath sounds, and blood pressure—to give students an authentic learning environment without putting any actual patients at risk.

Most students are drawn from the residency programs at Brigham and Women's and its affiliate hospitals and from emergency medical service agencies. But everyone doesn't have to crowd around a single simulator. The center is equipped with twenty-three machines, including four that simulate children's bodies.

Here, Dr. Sayon Dutta leads a class in basic airways techniques. The pace of emergency medicine, say the staff at STRATUS, bears little similarity to the flood of crises that confront doctors on nighttime broadcast television. While the simulators help students hone diagnostic and treatment skills, the hardest thing to learn in emergency medicine is communicating effectively and clearly during serious but uncommon events, establishing who is in charge, and working together to get the job done.

STRATUS works with the companies that manufacture these simulators to design new features and to use the simulators to test new medical devices as well. The success of the Brigham and Women's STRATUS Center has led to an expansion of the program, as Beth Israel and Boston Medical Center have established STRATUS programs of their own. The Brigham and Women's staff has also lent a hand consulting on similar training in Dubai, Kazakhstan, and India.

For information about the STRATUS program at Brigham and Women's Hospital, visit www.brighamandwomens.com/stratus.

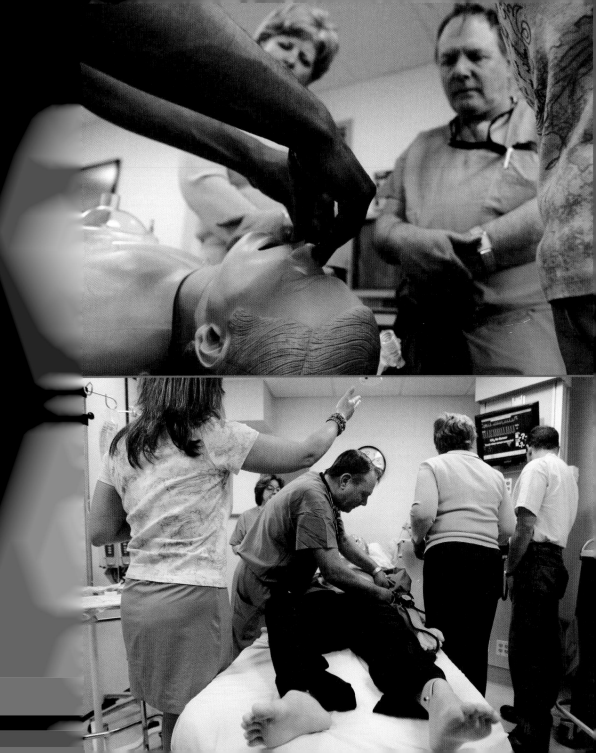

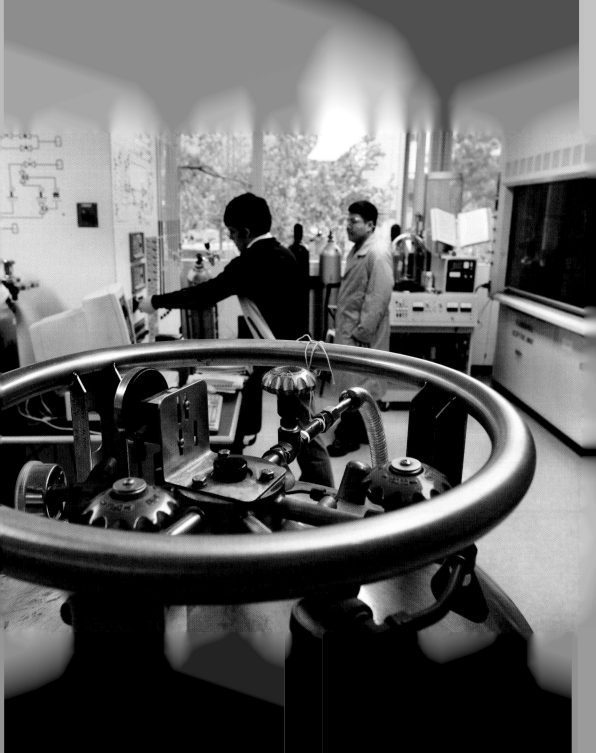

A Lil' Bit o' NASA
Northeastern University

When it was constructed in 1997, the Center for Advanced Microgravity Materials Processing (CAMMP) at Northeastern University was one of only a dozen NASA centers at major universities around the country. And it ranks only second in the history of science for experiments carried out on the Space Shuttle or the International Space Station—between four hundred and five hundred, according to Al Sacco Jr., CAMMP director and George A. Snell Distinguished Professor of Engineering at Northeastern. Most of those experiments dealt with understanding the crystallization of inorganic materials in low-gravity situations. One focus was on zeolites, a crystalline "molecular sieve" widely used to remove sulfur impurities in petroleum refining.

Sacco says that about fifty graduate students, fifteen to sixteen post-doctoral students, ten faculty, and about twenty undergraduates have participated in the research over the years. And while the center may be a NASA lab, few student researchers go on to the aerospace industry. Most end up working in materials science research with some of the center's industrial partners, which include DuPont and Allied Signal.

The lab is flying fewer experiments these days and conducting more on the ground. Its research embraces some cutting-edge science, such as growing gallium nitride crystals for environmental cleanup tasks in such low-light places as the deep ocean, underground mines, and outer space; creating quantum wire arrays to split water to produce hydrogen fuel; or growing field effect transistors in place with carbon nanotubes to produce extremely small and lightweight computing devices that consume very little power.

"Our research is all in nontraditional areas," Sacco says, "and there are no books on the subjects. Our students really have to learn to think outside the box. That's what the employers are looking for."

For more information on Northeastern's research for NASA, visit www.dac.neu.edu/cammp/.

Inside a Meat Locker
T. F. Kinnealey & Co.

Baby, it's cold inside. With storage for about 300,000 pounds of fresh meat, the Newmarket Square location of T. F. Kinnealey & Co. is one of New England's largest handlers of wholesale meat. During a typical week on the cutting floor, about thirty-five staff members process 100,000 pounds of meat. The cuts go to about a thousand customers all over eastern New England from Rhode Island to the Maine coast. Most of the product is either USDA choice or prime, and it includes the gamut of nonexotic meat: beef, pork, lamb, veal, and poultry.

According to company treasurer Joe Kinnealey, whose father and uncle started the business in 1939, things have changed radically in recent years. "With the meat-processing industry shifting to the Midwest," he says, "we get most of our meat in boxes now, instead of breaking down whole carcasses or sides." He also points out that the company cuts a lot of meat to order for hotels, restaurants, country clubs, and caterers. "Some restaurants still like to cut their own, especially if they're making unusual cuts," he says, "but having steaks precut guarantees exact portion control, a consistent product, and no waste." Steaks, in fact, are a signature Kinnealey product and are among its biggest sellers to customers like steakhouse Abe & Louie's. The company also supplies meat to some of the other top restaurants in greater Boston, such as Mistral, Blue Ginger, Rialto, and Locke-Ober.

At the company's Newmarket Square location, meatcutter David Hernandez handles one of those specialty steaks. Kinnealey says that the company trains almost all of its meat-cutters on the job because "there just aren't that many trained people around. Most of them work as butchers in the retail end."

To learn more about the butchers,
visit www.kinnealey.com

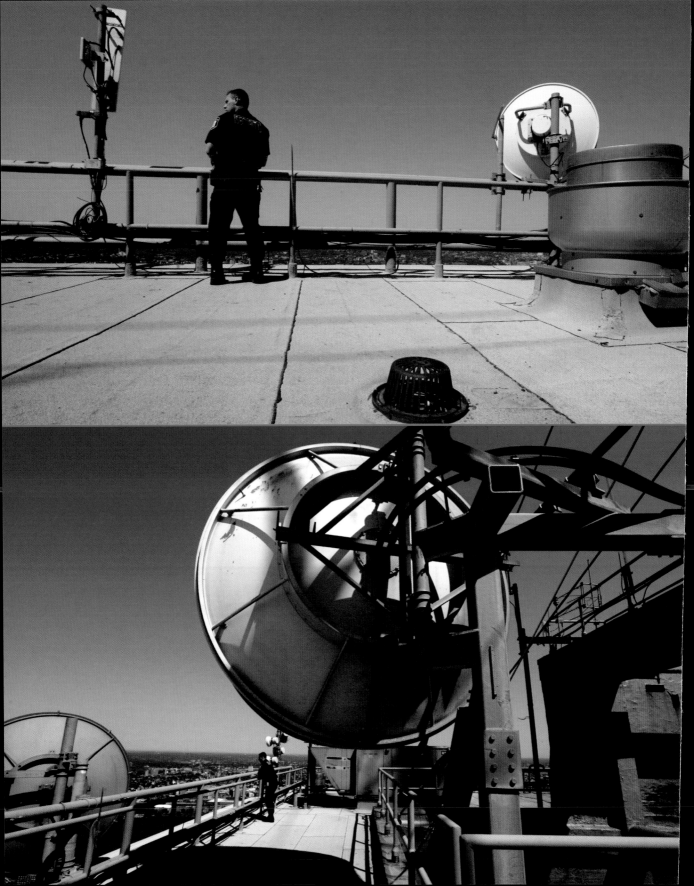

The "Real" Top of the Hub
The Prudential Tower

When it opened in 1964 as the tallest building in the city—and the tallest building in the world outside of New York—the Prudential Tower ushered in Boston's modern skyscraper era. Although the 759-foot Pru lost its local bragging rights to the 790-foot John Hancock Tower, completed in 1975, the fiftieth-floor Prudential Skywalk is said to be the highest public observation deck in Boston. Hungry thrill-seekers can also

ascend to the fifty-second floor to enjoy the view with a drink and a meal at the Top of the Hub restaurant.

But only authorized personnel, such as former security guard Kevin McDermott, are allowed on the open roof deck on the top of the building where they can look down at the city spread out below them. Even the John Hancock Tower seems dwarfed from this vantage point. Many afternoons, peregrine falcons perch atop the tower watching for small prey.

The Prudential Tower's boxy shape makes it a recognizable landmark on the Boston skyline—while the roof deck is a perfect place for mounting transmitting and communications equipment. The tallest antenna on the roof measures 153 feet and can be seen from twenty miles away. The tower's west-facing location has made it essential to the Boston Marathon. Every April a flurry of dish antennas and signal repeaters is mounted on the roof so that the race can be broadcast live on television.

Talk about a bird's-eye view!

The Skywalk Observatory & Exhibit is open seven days a week. For more information visit www.prudential center.com.

Watching for Fire
Department of Conservation and Recreation

Charlie Cicciu is more than up a tree—he's up over the trees as the observer in the Department of Conservation and Recreation (DCR) fire tower in Sharon, keeping an eye on the twenty-eight towns and cities that compose Norfolk County. Perched above two thousand acres belonging to DCR and the Massachusetts Audubon Society, the tower makes it possible to see up to one hundred miles away on a clear day. Just one of forty-three operational fire towers in the state (another thirteen are not functioning), it's part of a network of safety stations dating back to the nation's first fire tower, erected in Plymouth in 1886. The towers are staffed from about the end of March until late fall, or when the state gets enough relief from rain that the danger of fire is minimal. More than 85 percent of the state's fires are spotted from the towers.

According to Shawn Bush, District 7 fire warden, observers usually work eight-hour shifts in the towers, but their workdays can be extended whenever there's a high fire danger or fire frequency or when they're needed up high to facilitate

communications. The towers are rather minimalist work-spaces, equipped with two-way radios, phones, and weather radio. Some also have mini weather stations. For entertainment, a few observers listen to the radio. (They can't take their eyes off the forest to watch TV.) "Bathrooms" are located at ground level in the form of portable toilets.. Fire tower observer jobs are posted online under Mass.gov, and observers work anywhere from one season "to a whole career," says Bush.

Visitors are encouraged to climb the ninety steps to the Sharon tower's top. (Visitors are welcome at all the towers.) While he may credit the tower with supplying him with peace and solitude, Cicciu jumps at the opportunity to teach others about the dangers of fires and how to spot smoke from this secret perch above the trees.

For more information about the Massachusetts Department of Conservation and Recreation, visit its Web site at www .mass.gov/dcr.

Dining with Legends
Locke-Ober

If these walls could talk . . . It's almost impossible to imagine the conversations that have been held and the deals that have been sealed in the private dining rooms hidden away on the third floor of Locke-Ober. Its alleylike location near Downtown Crossing confounds many who search for the restaurant, but it's easy enough to find: Just look for the intersection of history and fine dining.

Although others operated less ambitious eateries on the spot, the Alsace-born Luis Ober pioneered gourmet dining on Winter Place. When he transformed his family's living quarters into six intimate dining rooms in the 1880s, he also remodeled the entry-level main dining room with lavish wood paneling and installed the humongous Reed & Barton silver soup tureens (lifted by a pulley system) that remain a fixture of Locke-Ober's decor. Even today, the genteel room persists as the place where Bostonians of a certain social class gather to see and be seen.

But for those who would rather not be seen, the John F. Kennedy room, which seats up to ten people, remains the most popular of the six private third-floor dining rooms. Kennedy would frequently meet here with advisers, politicos, and supporters, following the tradition of his grandfather John Fitzgerald. "Honey Fitz," who served as mayor of Boston in 1906–1908 and again in 1910–1914, often held meet-and-eat sessions at Locke-Ober.

Kennedy was particularly fond of Locke-Ober's lobster stew. According to restaurant spokeswoman Eve Piza, "He always drank the broth, but it's rumored that he gave the meat to the waiter." JFK's Lobster Stew remains on the menu—but we wonder if today's waiters are as lucky.

Locke-Ober is located at 3 Winter Place, near Downtown Crossing in Boston. For more information visit www.lockeober.com.

Saddling Up with the Mounted Police
Boston Police Department

Boston's peace officers have been trotting around the city at least since 1870, when the country's oldest mounted police unit was founded. (There's even good evidence that horseback policing in Boston may have begun as early as 1630. Apparently there was no room for a patrol car on the *Arbella*.) During the unit's heyday, more than one hundred steeds were housed in city stables. Now there are just a dozen or so at the police department's equine head-

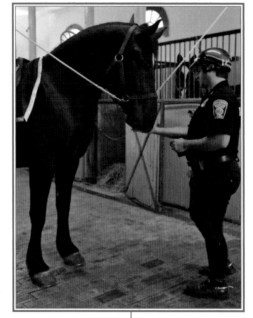

quarters at the Brandegee Estate in Jamaica Plain.

Sergeant Christopher Walsh supervises the ten officers in his unit. Patrol officers throughout the Boston Police Department are eligible to apply for the mounted unit, though inquiries outnumber openings by ten to one. "The main thing they need," says Walsh, "is to love the animals and not be afraid. These are big horses, and they're a challenge to someone with no riding experience."

New officers receive daily in-saddle training for twelve to fourteen weeks, working with the department's in-house trainer. Sergeant George Survillo (opposite) rides Bailey as he leads the morning training at the Boston Mounted Police riding facility. Boston police officer Joe Fawkes (left) gets ready to join him.

Each horse, Walsh says, has its own personality, but each has been trained to remain calm in the urban environment—to not be spooked by such things as fireworks or plastic bags blowing in the wind that might send most recreational mounts into a tizzy.

The average police horse spends ten years on the force, and the police department maintains a long list of people who want to adopt retiring horses. However, not all horses enter their sunset years dependent on the kindness of strangers. One mount has served twenty-six years in the unit, which should make it eligible for pension benefits.

For more information about the Boston Police Department, visit its Web site at www.cityofboston.gov/police/default.asp.

Grounding the Zakim
Boston Sand and Gravel Co.

Boston Sand and Gravel Co. has been in its Charlestown location next to the railroad tracks since the 1960s, when this section of Charlestown was an industrial area and the Big Dig was just a gleam in some demonic engineer's eye. Now it sits beneath one of the modern icons of Boston: the Leonard P. Zakim Bunker Hill Bridge.

"We kept operating right through the Big Dig," says company president Dean Boylan. "It was"—he pauses, looking for the right words— "very challenging, with all the construction around us. This one took a lot of logistics since they kept changing the access and egress points."

But Boston Sand and Gravel, after all, is in the construction business and took it all in stride. During the main construction season, the operation ships 100 to 150 loads of concrete daily. During the Big Dig, they produced even more, including some of the concrete for the Zakim Bridge.

"We're all proud to have played a part—really a very small part—in this beautiful new landmark for the city," Boylan says.

The company's trucks bear the slogan First and Finest, which Boylan says was given to them by one of their drivers many years ago. It is the motto of the Naval Mobile Construction Battalion 1, aka the Seabees.

Operations continue beneath the Zakim Bridge. Concrete sand, seen here, is shipped in from Ossipee, New Hampshire. The sand is moved into the processing plant on shuttle belts and mixed with gravel, cement, and water, then loaded directly into waiting trucks. The noise from the traffic passing overhead is intense—but that's to be expected when your workplace is underneath the widest cable-stayed bridge in the world.

Boston Sand and Gravel Co. is located at 100 North Washington Street. For more information about their services, visit www.bostonsand.com.

Meeting Eugene O'Neill
Shelton Hall, Boston University

When Boston University students are away for the summer, Suite 401 at Shelton Hall remains unoccupied. Or does it? Legend persists that this particular dormitory room is haunted by the ghost of Nobel Prize laureate playwright Eugene O'Neill, who died in the room in 1953. Over the years, the room's occupants have related tales of unexplained knocking on the walls and doors as well as the periodic flickering of lights.

"We're still charging him rent," jokes Phil Gloudemans, Boston University assistant vice president of media relations.

O'Neill came full circle. He was born in a hotel room on Times Square in New York (now the site of a Starbucks) and expired in a hotel room in Kenmore Square in Boston. Indeed, tradition has it that the author's final words were, "Born in a hotel room and, goddammit, died in one!" The building was constructed as one of the early Sheraton hotels. When local hoteliers bought the structure in 1950, they changed the name to "Shelton Hotel" so they could continue using the monogrammed linens and not have to replace the "S" on the building. Boston University bought the building in 1954 and converted it to dormitory rooms. In honor of O'Neill, the entire fourth floor houses students who have a concentration in writing.

They have big shoes to fill. On the fiftieth anniversary of O'Neill's death, the university installed a plaque at the building entrance, noting that he not only received the Nobel Prize for Literature in 1936 but was also awarded the Pulitzer Prize for Drama in 1920, 1922, 1928, and 1957. Displayed next to the plaque is a letter from his last wife, Carlotta, in which she wrote, "The Master is gone. I am alone."

Some residents of 401 might beg to differ.

Shelton Hall is located at 91 Bay State Road, Boston.

In honor of

Eugene Gladstone O'Neill

American playwright,
recipient of the Nobel Prize in Literature (1936)
and four Pulitzer Prizes for Drama (1920, 1922, 1928, 1957),
who died in suite 401 of the Hotel Shelton
at 91 Bay State Road
on November 27, 1953.

The first American dramatist to attain international recognition,
today he is considered our foremost playwright.

Office of Residence Life
Boston University
November 2003

Cruising in the State Police Corvette
Nashoba Valley Technical Institute

It might just be the flashiest looking vehicle in the fleet of the Massachusetts State Police—and it also happens to be the cheapest. When this 1989 Chevrolet Corvette was seized by detectives, it arrived at headquarters in deplorable condition. But it seemed a shame to let a once-fine muscle car go off to the automotive graveyard, so it became a reclamation project for students at the Nashoba Valley Technical Institute. The students labored over the car—how often do you get to work on a Vette in auto shop?—and managed to refurbish the vehicle in four months. They even hand-painted the shield emblazoned on the car's hood before they returned it to the state police in December 2003. Total price tag for the state? Zero dollars.

Before receiving its hood-to-tailpipes makeover from the Nashoba Valley Tech students, the car was a solid color and resembled any other Corvette on the road, according to the State Police garage. Officers used it for several years in undercover operations, fighting illegal drug trafficking, before the car received its current two-tone paint job. Today, it is used primarily "for public relations," says State Police trooper Michael Chavis of the Fleet Section. "We bring it to parades, if requested, and drive it for special events like the State Police Chase Road Race," a charity event. It might have been a hot car once upon a time, but, says Chavis, "It doesn't get driven all the time. It's pretty old."

For more information on the Massachusetts State Police Department, visit www.mass.gov.

Inspecting the E. Howard & Co. Clock
The Marriott Custom House

The E. Howard & Co. clock, located on the Marriott Custom House tower in downtown Boston, is one of the largest mechanical clocks in New England—and one of the fussiest. It became a fixture on the Boston skyline in 1915 when Boston's first skyscraper was created by adding a sixteen-story tower to the Greek Revival Custom House on State Street.

Alas, the clock's internal workings—its gears, pendulum, and motor—were built for a much smaller clock and did

not run properly in their prominent setting. Bostonians could not rely on their gigantic timepiece until 1987, when brothers David and Ross Hochstrasser, two clock enthusiasts, set out to fix it.

In 1997 the four twenty-five-foot diameter clock faces were refurbished to celebrate the opening of Marriott's Custom House luxury time-share condominiums. The work involved chipping and scraping out deteriorated concrete and painting the clock face. The wooden hands of the clock are covered with gold leaf, and the numbers and small minute circles are glass.

David Hochstrasser continues to take care of the clock. When winter snow and ice prevent the mechanism from working, Hochstrasser drives up from his South Shore home to reset the time. Making sure the clock is running properly is important to him. "It's a very historic building and it should be kept up."

Hochstrasser is not the only one to appreciate this distinctive building. In the spring, peregrine falcons often nest in the topmost window of the tower, facing the harbor. Visitors to the open-air observation deck on the twenty-sixth floor are often thrilled to see the swift little raptors rocket past. After visitors have enough of the jaw-dropping harbor and skyline views, they can stop on the twenty-fourth floor to have a firsthand look at the temperamental clock mechanism, safely ensconced behind glass.

The Custom House is located at 3 McKinley Square, Boston. The observation deck is open for limited tours Monday through Saturday. For more information visit www.marriott .com.

Going Nowhere on the Red Line
The Massachusetts Bay Transportation Authority

The underground city has been the stuff of urban legend at least since French novelist Gaston Leroux set his gothic romance, *Phantom of the Opera*, beneath the streets of Paris. Rome has its catacombs, New York its alligator-infested sewers. And Boston has its superseded subterranean train stations—the last stops to nowhere on the oldest subway system in North America.

Passengers riding the Red Line from Central Square to Harvard Station have the opportunity to spy a piece of transportation history. Just as the brakes start to screech, they can look closely on the right side to see the ghostly remains of the old platform east of the current Harvard Station. The station was closed after the Alewife extension opened in the early 1980s. Travelers can also catch a glimpse of the now defunct Harvard-Holyoke Station, on the right side of inbound trains, just after leaving Harvard Station. The cavernous tunnel seen here (opposite, top) was the old

terminus and turnaround beneath Brattle Street. Mark Marcarelli (in green shirt), a project superintendent with O'Connor Company, and Pat Hynes (red shirt), a mechanical engineer with the T, survey the area.

Broadway Station in South Boston has a similar tale. Until 1919, Broadway Station had another connection platform one level above the subway station. Subway riders could connect to T streetcars via free transfers and emerge aboveground. After the extension to Andrew Square was built, the tunnel seen here (opposite, below) was decommissioned. Hynes and Marcarelli inspect the space, which is directly under West Broadway in South Boston.

Judging by the recent graffiti, the station might be abandoned, but not forgotten.

To view MBTA maps and learn more about the country's oldest subway system, visit www.mbta.com/ schedules_and_maps/subway/.

Off the Ice:
Inside the Bruins' Locker Room
TD Banknorth Garden

Keith Robinson has seen a lot of black-and-gold laundry in more than two decades as an assistant equipment manager for the Boston Bruins. Unlike most of the players, he even remembers when the Garden was the Garden—a sweaty little building full of glorious memories—instead of a nice, bright, spacious structure with immaculate dressing rooms and unobscured sight lines from the seats.

With the Bruins playing some forty home games (at least), plus a bunch of preseason events, Robinson has his hands full. Among his many chores, he has to organize the locker rooms for both the home and away teams. He's no stranger to getting up close and personal with the members

of the team. Here he carefully folds socks for the Bruins in their TD Banknorth Garden locker room. It might sound like a mundane chore, but even the most aggressive high-sticker can be laid low by a blister from wrinkled socks.

Robinson is the man who sees to the details—making sure the sticks are taped, the jerseys are washed, skates are repaired, and the locker room is stocked with everything from practice pucks to chewing gum for the players.

It's a lot of work to make it easy for a bunch of grown men to play.

The Bruins play home games at TD Banknorth Garden on Causeway Street, Boston. For more information visit http://bruins.nhl.com.

Riding WBZ's Traffic Helicopter
Above Greater Boston

WACK-A . . . WACK-A . . . WACK-A . . . WACK-A . . . Commuters hear the sound above them as they sit in line in their vehicles, waiting to get off the Tobin Bridge or at least to the South Station mouth of the expressway tunnel. And if they tune their radios to 1030 on the AM band (remember AM? Before satellite radio, before FM ...), they might even hear the, well, not-so-dulcet tones of traffic reporter Joe Morgan

telling them what they now know from experience. (That's why you're supposed to listen to the traffic report *before* heading out.)

WBZ was Boston's first radio station back in the 1920s, and it has been presenting "traffic on the threes" from its traffic helicopter for more than forty years. Known simply as "the WBZ copter," the Robinson-44 craft is smaller than most other traffic helicopters. Each morning, traffic reporter

Joe Morgan flies from Beverly down Route 1 into Boston, out along the Expressway, in above Route 128, and out again over the Massachusetts Turnpike. Morgan is just the latest of a series of 'BZ chopper jockeys, having moved into the slot in 1997. The North Shore native says he "loves to slip the surly bonds of earth every morning and afternoon and give our listeners/drivers real-time survival information."

Scrappy and difficult to spot from the ground, the copter flies at an altitude between five hundred and one thousand feet to cover traffic and news stories. Barring high winds or low visibility, trust that the WBZ copter is somewhere above that parking lot called the Expressway. Surly bonds indeed.

For more information visit WBZ's Web site at http://wbztv.com.

The Secret Gardens of Beacon Hill
Beacon Hill Garden Club

"Full many a flower is born to blush unseen," Thomas Gray wrote in "Elegy Written in a Country Churchyard." In fact, he penned that thought just about the time that the real estate developers were turning John Hancock's pasture into Beacon Hill. As the homes went up on smaller and smaller lots, they created a warren of hidden backyards—and hidden gardens where many a posy, indeed, blushes unseen.

Unless the garden happens to be on that year's tour of the Beacon Hill Garden Club. Once a year in May since 1930, garden enthusiasts have been able to catch a glimpse of these urban landscapes during the Beacon Hill Garden Club hidden garden tour. The tour takes the public down private alleyways, pathways, and sometimes into residents' homes.

Paula O'Keeffe, a club member who coordinated the hidden garden tour for several years, says there are about four dozen active gardens among the members, including the Brimmer Street

garden tended by Rogina Jeffries. The gardens range from patches as small as ten by twenty feet to a large garden that measures thirty by forty feet. Some residents hire landscape architects to design a professional garden, while others create floral sanctuaries on their own.

While most Beacon Hill gardens are fairly diminutive, they can be expensive to plant and maintain. "Shade is the biggest challenge, but some people just love horticulture," says O'Keeffe. "They keep putting out different flowering plants to see what will live."

The gardens tend to reflect the personality of the gardener, according to O'Keeffe. "One of our members was married to a modern architect, so the inside of their house was spare and lean. But her garden was a mass of color and detail—that's where she expressed her taste."

For information on the Beacon Hill Garden Tour, visit www.beaconhillgardenclub.org.

Exploring Acela's Cockpit
Amtrak's Acela Train

The most striking thing about the cockpit of Amtrak's Acela is its simplicity. Although the train is one of the most sophisticated examples of third-generation high-speed rail, its subdued dashboard display is complemented by only a handful of levers, switches, and buttons. That's all it takes to control the potentially fastest train in North America. The Acela (a name that was an adman's enjambment of "acceleration" and "excellence") is built to achieve a top speed of 150 miles per hour on its journeys between Boston, New York, and Washington, D.C. Thanks to limitations of the train's ability to tilt on curves and the condition of much of the track along the Northeast Corridor, the actual average speed is 86 miles per hour.

After years of planning for high-speed rail in the United States, Amtrak awarded the Acela Express contract to a consortium of train builders led by the Canadian firm Bombardier (which

also builds many of the cars for Boston's MBTA system). Another partner in the consortium, Alstom, was the French manufacturer of the two-hundred-mile-per-hour TGV trains that have supplanted air travel on many French routes. Amtrak stipulated that the Acela had to be built largely on U.S. soil, so most of the construction was carried out in Bombardier plants in Barre, Vermont, and Plattsburgh, New York.

High-speed rail service on the Northeast Corridor began in December 2000, and while the Acela trains were sidelined briefly in 2004 to have their brake systems redesigned, there's been no looking back ever since. More than ten million passengers have traveled on the fleet of twenty Acela Express trains.

All aboard!

For more information on the Acela, visit Amtrak's Web site at www.amtrak.com.

Feeding the Lions
Franklin Park Zoo

Wednesday is "fast day" for certain birds and beasts at the Franklin Park Zoo. Instead of their usual meat diets, both the Andean condors and the African lions get bones to pick.

As far as Tito and Inti, the male and female condors, respectively, are concerned, "bone day" is their favorite day of the week. As carrion eaters, the gigantic birds enjoy tugging and ripping at the bits of cartilage left on the bones and are adept at using their beaks to hollow out the bones and eat the marrow. The other six days of the week, the condors eat about a pound and

a half per day of a special meat diet formulated for birds of prey. They are fed between 1:00 and 4:00 p.m., and zoo visitors are welcome to watch. The female tends to get especially close to the keepers, as she was hand-raised as a chick.

Christopher, the four-hundred-pound African male lion shown here with Charlotte Speakman, has been a resident of the Franklin Park Zoo since 2001. Except for Wednesday, the king of beasts gets the zoo equivalent of room service. His diet consists of eleven pounds of horsemeat augmented with dietary supplements, divided into two meals a day. The first feeding is early in the morning before he goes into the exhibit enclosure, the second after he comes off exhibit in the evening. That way, zookeepers need never enter the holding areas with the big cats.

All the lions and tigers get only bones on Wednesday. "Because in the wild they wouldn't typically eat every day," explains zookeeper Speakman, "we give them a fast day when they just receive bones to maintain a healthy digestive system and healthy set of teeth."

Franklin Park Zoo is at One Franklin Park Road in Dorchester. For more information visit www.franklinparkzoo.org.

Raising a Glass
Cheers Pub

It may be known around the globe as the bar "where everybody knows your name," but few Bostonians would make that claim. The Bull & Finch Pub, founded in 1969, lost many regulars when it officially changed its name in 2001 to Cheers, assuming the identity of the television show that had been loosely modeled after the cozy Boston bar. Even though production of new episodes of the show ended in 1993, the popularity of the bar remains undaunted, thanks to reruns and the allure of finding a welcoming watering hole.

Each year, more than 750,000 customers squeeze into the cramped quarters of the original location of Cheers in the basement of the Hampshire House on Beacon Hill (shown in the TV show's opening credits) and its newer Faneuil Hall branch—but precious few are Bostonians unless they have out-of-town guests in tow. Director of marketing Gail Richman says 95 percent of customers are tourists, but that "locals tend to still visit us in the slower winter months."

But even locals who've sat down for a Giant Norm Burger or Carla's Roast Beef at Cheers are unlikely to have gotten a backstage peek at the famous restaurant. The bar looks familiar—after all, designers used photos of the original Bull & Finch to create the *Cheers* set. But the kitchen is a frenzy of activity with eighteen staff working under executive chef Markus Ripperger to produce an average of 4,365 meals a month. A native of Zurich, Ripperger has been with the Hampshire House since 1992, balancing private-party meals and the public summer Sunday jazz brunch in the Library upstairs at the Hampshire House with traditional pub fare that stays true to the show's theme and the Bull & Finch's heritage. Just don't expect to find too many lost Bostonians wandering into the kitchen, asking where the gift shop is.

Cheers is located at 84 Beacon Street, Boston. For more information visit www.cheersboston.com.

Visiting a Nuclear Reactor
Massachusetts Institute of Technology

Few people beyond the intersection of Massachusetts Avenue and Albany Street in Cambridge have a clue that a five-megawatt nuclear reactor sits in their midst—smack-dab in the center of a municipality that declares itself a "nuclear-free zone." But the small nuclear facility, which has been on the Massachusetts Institute of Technology campus for more than half a century, is hardly the stuff of Three Mile Island or Chernobyl. For one thing, the reactor's design doesn't allow operating temperatures above 120 degrees Fahrenheit—about the temperature of a home hot water heater. And it produces less than $\frac{1}{600}$ the power of a typical nuclear plant in the electric grid.

The reactor serves as a research facility for MIT scientists, as well as for high school and college students. The main research programs focus on designing the next generation of nuclear power reactors and fuels. Among the recent discoveries at the MIT facility were ways to make nuclear fuel even more efficient, thus cutting down on nuclear

waste. Researchers at the MIT reactor also study nuclear medicine and the treatment of cancer with radioisotopes.

MIT has worked to educate the Cambridge community about the safety of the facility, even in the unlikely event that something happens to the reactor. After the events of September 11, 2001, the university eliminated all storage of enriched uranium. David Moncton, director of the nuclear reactor laboratory, told *The Boston Globe* that the uranium retained on-site is "about one-tenth what you would need to make a bomb, and every time we get a shipment, the fuel rods are put immediately into the reactor in a tank that's under a 20,000-ton lid that you need a crane to open."

MIT's nuclear reactor is located at the intersection of Massachusetts Avenue and Albany Street. For more information visit www.mit.edu.

Credits

Boston.com editor:
David Beard

Features editor:
Ron Agrella

Original concept and online project editor:
Christine Makris

Overview writers:
Patricia Harris and David Lyon

Writers/reporters:
Christopher Brook, Meghan Colloton, Nicole Duarte, Christine Makris, Jennifer Nelson, Bianca Strzelczyk, Eric Wilbur, Glenn Yoder

Photo editor:
Leanne Burden Seidel

Primary photographers:
John Tlumacki, ii, 4–5, 8–9, 10–11, 12–13, 14–15, 18–19, 20–21, 24–25, 26–27, 30–31, 46–47, 52–53, 54–55, 80–81, 82–83, 84–85, 91; Jonathan Wiggs, i, viii, xii–1, 2–3, 6–7, 16–17, 22–23, 28–29, 34–35, 36, 38–39, 44–45, 48–49, 50–51, 56–57, 58–59, 60–61, 62–63, 64–65, 66–67, 68–69, 70–71, 72–73, 74–75, 76–77, 78–79, 88–89, 92–93, 94–95, 96–97

Additional photography:
Yoon S. Byun, ix; Dominic Chavez, 83, 98–99; Jim Davis, 37; Justine Hunt, xi; Janet Knott, 86–87; Michele McDonald, 42–43; Evan Richman, 40–41; David L. Ryan, 83; Essdras M Suarez, 82–83; Mark Wilson, 32–33, 83; Mark Micheli, i, 90; Chitose Suzuki, 30–31; UPI, x

The Boston Globe and Boston.com are the recognized leaders in providing in-depth, comprehensive, relevant news and information to the Boston area.

Day in and day out, the Globe's award-winning reporters and photographers cover the neighborhoods, people, and innerworkings of one of America's most beloved cities. Their strong connection to the life of the city and region has allowed them to discover and now share fascinating places known only to very few. *The Boston Globe* is wholly owned by The New York Times Company.